Audubon MINNESOTA
AN AUDUBON BIRDING GUIDE

The North Shore Birding Trail

A Guide to Birding Minnesota's North Shore of
Lake Superior from Duluth to Grand Portage

ACKNOWLEDGMENTS

The North Shore Birding Trail is a project of Audubon Minnesota. Thank you to the following individuals who generously shared their time and expertise:

- Dave Benson
- David S. Carman
- Kim Eckert
- Laura Erickson
- Jan Green
- Anthony Hertzel
- Molly & Ken Hoffman
- Bob Janssen
- Jim Lind
- Sue McDonnell

Photographers

- Micheal Furtman
- MN DNR, Carrol Henderson
- David Hundrieser

Cover Photos: Rough-legged Hawk, © michaelfurtman.com
Split Rock Lighthouse, © David Hundrieser
Scarlet Tanager, © MN DNR, Carrol Henderson

Audubon Minnesota Project Coordinators

Project Director – Mark Martell, Director of Bird Conservation
Project Coordinator and Editor – Bonnie K. Hundrieser, Director of Education

Graphic Design

Katie Clapp, Clapp Media Works

Funding for this project was provided by the Minnesota Environment and Natural Resources Trust Fund as recommended by the Legislative Commission on Minnesota Resources (LCMR). Proceeds from the sale of this guide will be used to fund future editions of this guide.

Audubon MINNESOTA

Printed on 10% post-consumer recycled paper.

CONTENTS

Palisade Head

FOREWORD

Audubon Minnesota: Our History and Mission

Audubon Minnesota, established in 1979, is the state office of the National Audubon Society. Working in cooperation with the Audubon-Mississippi River Headwaters to Gulf Program, we share Audubon's 100-year heritage of working to protect our environment, as well as the Audubon mission:

to conserve and restore natural ecosystems, focusing on birds, other wildlife, and their habitats

We operate in the belief that every person can make a difference and that people acting together can meet any challenge. As part of the National Audubon Society, we establish statewide programs and pursue funding to support important conservation efforts in Minnesota. Our nearly 10,000 Minnesota members, working in their communities, belong to 14 affiliated Audubon chapters across the state.

Our Goals

Audubon Minnesota's work is strategically focused on accomplishing four goals:

1. Stabilize or increase populations of at-risk bird species

2. Prevent declines in numbers and range area of common native birds

3. Protect and restore essential sites for vulnerable bird species

4. Improve and protect the health of landscapes that support or could support Minnesota birds

Audubon Minnesota Chapters

To learn about Audubon in Minnesota or the Audubon-Mississippi Headwaters to Gulf Program and for contact names and phone numbers of a Minnesota chapter near you, call the Audubon Minnesota office at 651-739-9332 or visit http://mn.audubon.org.

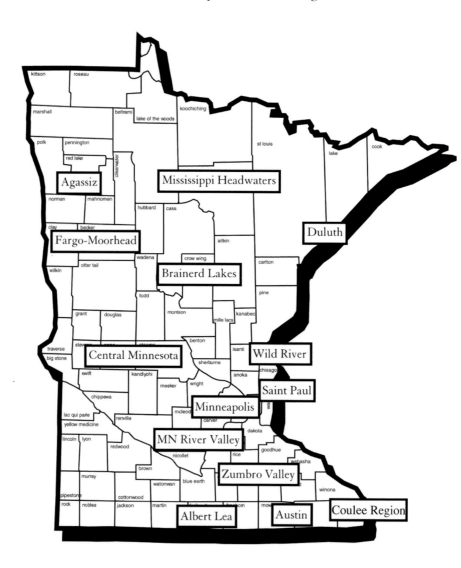

Audubon Important Bird Areas

Identifying & Conserving Essential Habitat for Birds

© michaelfurtman.com

The Important Bird Areas Program was initiated in the 1980s by BirdLife International in Europe. In the U.S., Audubon is the partner to BirdLife and is responsible for implementing the Important Bird Area Program. Country by country across the globe BirdLife partners are involved in the identification and conservation of the most important places for birds. Once identified, Important Bird Areas become the focus of a grassroots conservation effort involving birdwatchers, land conservationists, community leaders, landowners and individuals. Galvanized around the realization that habitat destruction and degradation are the major threats to birds and other wildlife, these citizen conservationists focus attention on ensuring that Important Bird Areas are protected, properly managed, and that the threats to these sites are minimized.

Peregrine Falcon

The Audubon Minnesota Important Bird Areas Program, begun in 2003, is a partnership with the Minnesota Department of Natural Resources Nongame Program. With Audubon and the MN DNR at the helm, organizations from across the state are being brought together to assist with the identification and conservation of Minnesota's Important Bird Areas.

To learn how to participate or for more information on the Audubon Important Bird Area Program visit www.audubon.org/bird/iba. Here you will find a listing of Minnesota's Important Bird Areas and details on the threats and conservation actions that are happening at these sites.

For information about Audubon Minnesota's Important Bird Area Program, contact:

Audubon Minnesota
(651) 739-9332
mnaudubon@audubon.org

INTRODUCTION

Welcome to the North Shore of Lake Superior!

The North Shore Birding Trail guide was created to highlight the best places for bird watching between Duluth and Grand Portage, focusing on Highway 61 as the main route of the trail. As you travel the North Shore, you will experience birding along rugged cliffs, wide vistas of Lake Superior, beautiful state parks with spectacular waterfalls and hiking trails, and charming North Shore communities with excellent hospitality services. During any season, the North Shore is an exciting place to explore.

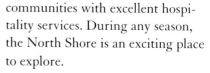

To Use this Guide

Refer to the numbered sites on the maps throughout the guide for the location, description and bird species you may find at that site at different times throughout the year. A bird checklist is provided for you to record your sightings.

PLEASE NOTE: Locations for many of the birding sites along the North Shore are referenced by mile markers on Hwy. 61 (see parentheses in the "Location" paragraph of a site description). Mile 0 is in Duluth (at the corner of London Road and 10th Ave. East); mile 71 is at the county line dividing Lake and Cook counties, and mile 150 is the Canadian border. If a location is given as mile 52.4, for example, it is 0.4 mile north of mile maker 52, or 0.6 mile south of mile marker 53.

© David Hundrieser

A Unique Land for Habitat & Birds: Minnesota's Northwoods

Minnesota has become nationally known for the bird watching opportunities that exist in the northeast region because of the presence of species such as Great Gray Owl, Boreal Owl, Northern Hawk-Owl, Philadelphia Vireo, Black-throated Blue Warbler, Connecticut Warbler, Spruce Grouse, and Bohemian Waxwing. Fall and spring migrations of raptors, songbirds, waterfowl and owls along the western tip of Lake Superior are some of nature's most incredible events in the region.

When people imagine the northwoods of Minnesota, more than likely they are thinking about the Laurentian Mixed Forest eco-province. It is the largest of the four eco-provinces of Minnesota, covering two-fifths of the state. It consists of a mixture of white spruce, balsam fir, and pines interspersed with stands of aspen and birch. Its topography is comprised largely of rolling hills. This area, also known as the northern boreal forest, is home to both the highest and lowest points in the state. Glaciers sculpted this landscape, leaving relatively thin deposits of till blanketing the bedrock in the northeast and deeper deposits in the southern and western portions. Boulders, outcrops, hills, numerous lakes, bogs and vast tracks of forestland comprise this much-loved eco-province. The state's iron ranges also occur here. Dense forests occupy the uplands, with bedrock lakes in the northeast, ice block lakes in the south and west, and large, open peatlands in north central Minnesota. This eco-province provides much of the critical natural habitats that many boreal bird and wildlife species depend upon.

© MN DNR, Carrol Henderson

Great Gray Owl

Bird Species of Conservation Concern in Minnesota

430 bird species have been recorded in Minnesota. With limited time and resources available to protect them, it is vital to know which species are at greatest risk. It is especially important to identify at-risk species before their populations become so small that protecting them from extinction is costly, in every sense of the word. Audubon Minnesota has identified 84 Species of Conservation Concern. These include State or Federally listed Endangered, Threatened or Special Concern species, those listed on the Audubon Watch List, and species whose populations are declining, particularly vulnerable, or in need of special monitoring or management attention.

Throughout the North Shore Birding Trail Guide you will find profiles that highlight some of these species of Conservation Concern that depend on the habitats found in northeast Minnesota. Many of these species fall under the watchful eye of "conservation concern" because of their limited range in the state. With such sensitivity to habitat needs, many species are susceptible to the effects of habitat fragmentation resulting from development and some logging practices, both in their breeding and wintering territories. Since these more rare species are often those sought by birders, Audubon encourages all birders to take special care to respect and protect these birds, and their habitats. We have a special responsibility to ensure their continued survival.

© MN DNR, Carrol Henderson

Northern Shrike

Explore Opportunities for Boreal Birding

If you are in search of birding in the boreal forests of northeast Minnesota, you are encouraged to explore the numerous roads that lead inland, away from Lake Superior, into the northwoods. Watch for the following recommended routes highlighted on the map, and use a Minnesota DeLorme Atlas to help explore these routes and their connecting side roads.

Lake County Road 2 – 46 miles
(See map site 21, page 24; description, page 27)

Sawbill Trail (Cook County Road 2) – 25 miles
(See map site 38, page 36; description, page 40)
From the town of Tofte, head north on County Road 2. Watch for breeding songbirds in spring and summer, and in winter watch for grouse and raptors, and listen for owls.

Caribou Trail (Cook County Road 4) – 20 miles
(See map site 41, page 36; description, page 41)
Beginning on the shore just east of Lutsen, follow the Caribou Trail north to The Grade (County Road 170). Drive east and return to Grand Marais via County Road 158. Along the way, visit Thompson Falls and climb Eagle Mountain, the highest point in Minnesota. In winter, watch for Ruffed or Spruce grouse along the trail, and stop along the route to listen to owls.

Gunflint Trail (Cook County Road 12) – 58 miles
(See map site 45, page 36; description, page 46)

© MN DNR, Carrol Henderson

Arrowhead Trail (Cook County Road 16) – 18 miles
(See map site 50, page 48; description, page 50)
Just east of Hovland, follow County Road 16 north up to the eastern edges of the Boundary Waters Canoe Area Wilderness.

Common Loon

Birding the Back Country: Hike the Superior Hiking Trail

The Superior Hiking Trail is a 205 mile-long footpath that follows the spectacular rocky North Shore ridgeline above Lake Superior in northeastern Minnesota. It begins just north of Two Harbors and ends just before the Canadian border. The trail has 30 trailheads and 81 backcountry campsites making it ideal for both day hikes and back-packing. In addition, the Superior Hiking Trail Association is working to complete an additional 40 miles of trail through the forests and ridges of Duluth. There are no fees, reservations or permits required to hike or backpack on the trail. Trail maps are available at all information centers and many resorts. The Superior Hiking Trail can be accessed from all state parks and inland crossroads. For more information contact the Superior Hiking Trail Association at 218-834-2700, or email: suphike@mr.net or visit www.shta.org.

© David Hundrieser

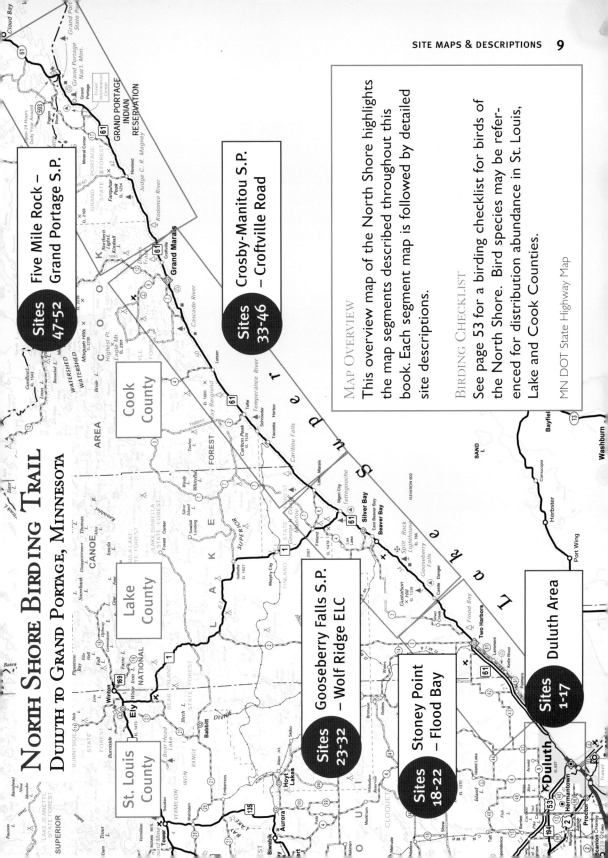

North Shore Birding Trail
Duluth to Grand Portage, Minnesota

Map Overview

This overview map of the North Shore highlights the map segments described throughout this book. Each segment map is followed by detailed site descriptions.

Birding Checklist

See page 53 for a birding checklist for birds of the North Shore. Bird species may be referenced for distribution abundance in St. Louis, Lake and Cook Counties.

MN DOT State Highway Map

Sites 47-52 — Five Mile Rock – Grand Portage S.P.

Sites 33-46 — Crosby-Manitou S.P. – Croftville Road

Sites 23-32 — Gooseberry Falls S.P. – Wolf Ridge ELC

Sites 18-22 — Stoney Point – Flood Bay

Sites 1-17 — Duluth Area

St. Louis County

Lake County

Cook County

DULUTH AREA

SITES 1-17

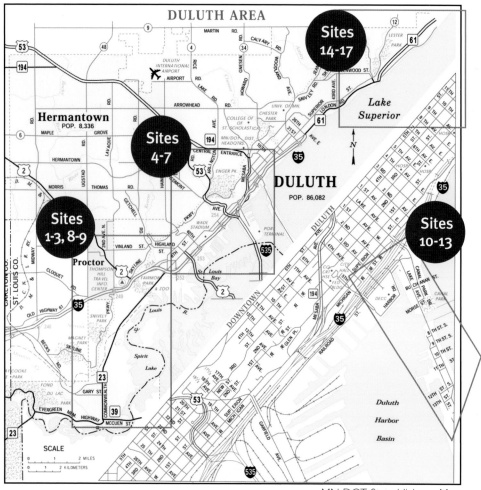

MN DOT State Highway Map

ST. LOUIS RIVER AND ESTUARY
1. Grassy Point Trail
2. Western Waterfront Trail
3. Boy Scout Landing
4. Port Terminal/Interstate Island
5. The Erie Pier Area
6. Garfield Avenue

WEST SKYLINE PARKWAY
7. Primary Count Site
8. Secondary Count Site
9. Bardon's Peak Overlook

PARK POINT/MINNESOTA POINT
10. Canal Park
11. Hearding Island
12. Park Point Recreation Area
13. Sky Harbor Airport

14. HAWK RIDGE NATURE RESERVE

LESTER PARK AREA
15. Lester Park/Lester River Mouth
16. Brighton Beach
17. Lakewood Pumping Station

DULUTH AREA

SITES 1-3, 8-9

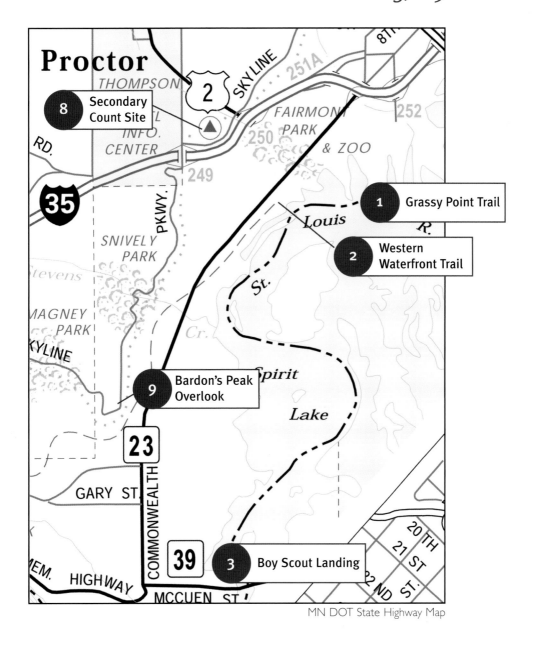

MN DOT State Highway Map

DULUTH AREA

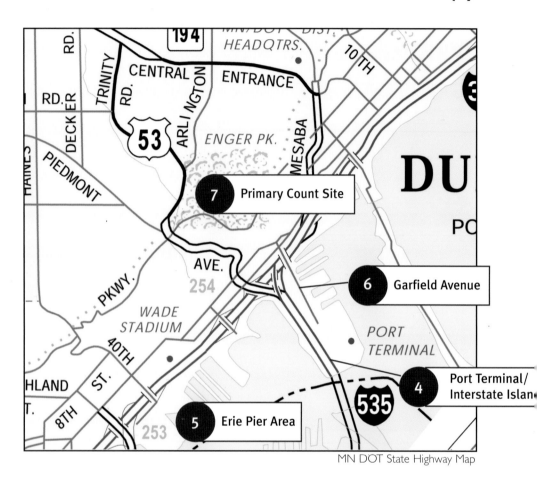

MN DOT State Highway Map

DULUTH AREA   SITES 10-13

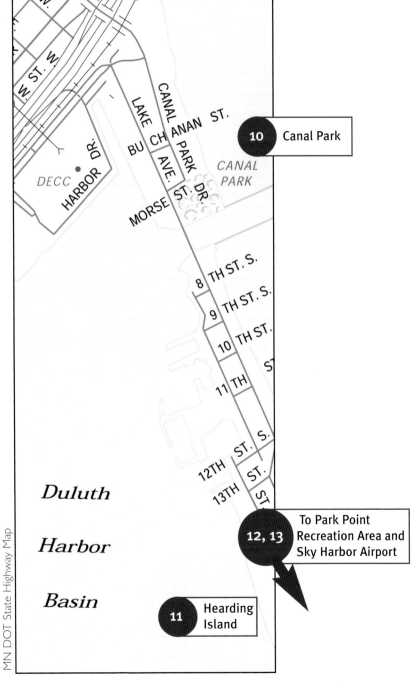

10 Canal Park

12, 13 To Park Point Recreation Area and Sky Harbor Airport

11 Hearding Island

MN DOT State Highway Map

DULUTH AREA

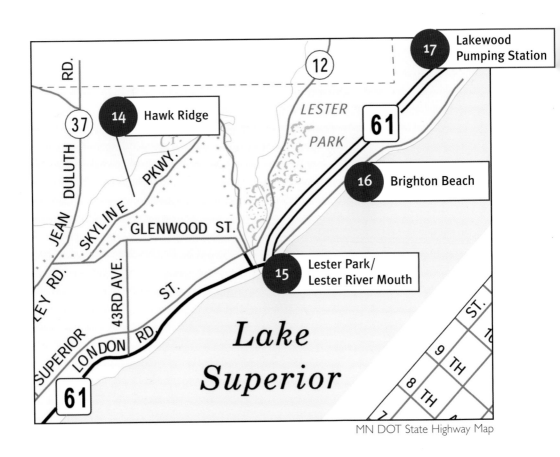

MN DOT State Highway Map

ST. LOUIS RIVER & ESTUARY AREA   SITES 1-6

DESCRIPTION   The St. Louis River estuary provides excellent birding opportunities all year around. The St. Louis River, after passing through Jay Cooke State Park, goes under State Highway 23 at its junction with State Highway 210 near Fond du Lac and begins to slow and to widen as it makes its final passage to Lake Superior. Between Fond du Lac and the Duluth Harbor the estuary has relatively little shoreline development (especially on the Wisconsin side), and the riparian vegetation gives way to mostly deciduous tree cover; this, combined with its southwest-to-northeast orientation from New Duluth to Lake Superior, many mid-stream islands and several marshy areas make it an attractive corridor for migrating birds, as well as providing abundant nesting habitat.

LOCATION   Located at the western edge of Lake Superior. Directions for numerous birding opportunities in the river/estuary area are provided below.

BIRDS   Large flocks of migrating water-fowl in early spring (late March – early May) spend time resting and feeding while waiting for ice-out farther north. The estuary is the best spot in northeast Minnesota to view Tundra Swans (late March – late April). Birders can spot many raptors flying overhead as they make their way over the shore to the north. May brings the majority of the passerine species, with the warblers coming through in waves beginning around the third week. The best way to appreciate the birdlife of the estuary is to take advantage of the many access points where one can either stop and view open areas, or else hike slowly along the shore. Several areas are recommended.

bird profile

American Black Duck

The American Black Duck nests in freshwater and brackish wetlands, and is known to be one of the most wary and quickest of ducks. Their diet includes insects, worms, snails, aquatic vegetation, seeds, grass, forbs, berries, and also grain. Populations have been in a long decline from habitat loss, pollution problems, and competition from Mallards. The two species frequently hybridize and this is thought to be another source of the American Black Duck decline. This bird winters within North America.

© michaelfurtman.com

1 **Grassy Point Trail** A marsh boardwalk that extends into the river near the Hwy. 2 bridge, on the Minnesota side. Interpretive signs along the trail enhance the birding experience. To get there, take Raleigh St. east off Grand Ave. (Hwy. 23), just south of I-35 and go 1.1 miles on Raleigh to the intersection with Lesure, then turn left and go to the end of the road. The trailhead is clearly marked there.

2 **Western Waterfront Trail** One-half mile farther southwest on Grand Avenue is 71st Ave. W, where the LS&M (Lake Superior & Mississippi) train boards. Just south of that is the Willard Munger Inn, at 75th Ave. W and there is a parking lot behind the motel, on 75th, where birders can park to hike the trail along the river at Indian Point, a public campground. This might be the most birded spot in west Duluth. Many birders take the "loop" around Indian Point for good viewing opportunities of warblers and waterfowl.

3 **Boy Scout Landing** Located just south of the Hwy. 39/Grand Ave. intersection, at the point where Grand Ave. (Hwy. 23) bends to the west (6.5 miles from I-35). This is a public boat launch area that provides a view of a wide section of the river. A more elevated view of the river can be had by driving a couple tenths of a mile west on Hwy. 23 to the marked Scenic Lookout. This is a good place to set up a spotting scope to look for swans, pelicans, and ducks in spring.

4 **Port Terminal/Interstate Island** One of the best places in winter to scan the buildings and bay ice for Snowy Owls and Gyrfalcons is from the Port Terminal. From the Garfield Avenue – Port Terminal exit off of Interstate 535, go straight and then bear left past the UPS building, bear right at the T, and drive to the edge of the bay opposite Hearding Island. If you turn right at the sign just west of the UPS building you'll shortly come to some good places to scan the bay ice and spots from which to scan Interstate Island. In spring and summer watch for Common and Caspian terns, Bonaparte's Gulls and migrant shorebirds.

© michaelfurtman.com

Sharp-shinned Hawk

5 **The Erie Pier Area** can be rewarding during migration, when you can scan the harbor for herons, waterfowl, shorebirds, gulls and terns. Often a good assortment of passerines are attracted to the trees and weedy flats, especially warblers, sparrows, pipits, longspurs and Snow Buntings. To get there, take the 40th Avenue west exit off Interstate 35, cross to the frontage road on the bay side of the freeway, park outside the gate and follow the gravel road, which leads to the right just beyond the frontage road. Walk up to the levee, which encloses a large pool and mudflats where dredge material from the harbor is deposited. Note that fluctuating water levels will affect bird species.

6 **Garfield Avenue** is great for winter birding, and parallels Interstate 535 from the Port Terminal exit to Superior Street. Check any of its connecting side streets and scan the grain elevators and railroad yards, where spilled grain attracts mice, rats and Rock Pigeons. These in turn annually attract a few Snowy Owls. This is the most consistent place in the state to find this species. The best time to look for owls is at dawn or late in the afternoon when they are most actively hunting or perching. Birders should respect signs for the surrounding private properties.

Snowy Owl

© MN DNR, Carrol Henderson

WEST SKYLINE PARKWAY   SITES 7-9

DESCRIPTION   During the spring raptor migration period (roughly March 1 to the end of May) the topography of West Duluth in combination with the funneling effect of the south shore of Lake Superior, concentrates raptor, passerine and other migrants along the ridges above the Duluth-Superior Harbor.

Rough-legged Hawk

LOCATION   The West Skyline Hawk Count (a spring raptor count) has been conducted since 1997 from two locations along West Skyline Parkway in West Duluth. Locations for three main areas are provided below.

BIRDS   Impressive numbers of Bald and Golden Eagles in March, Red-tailed and Rough-legged Hawks follow in mid-April, Turkey Vultures, Ospreys, Sharp-shinned Hawks, American Kestrels and finally Broad-winged Hawks follow in late April to May.

(7) **The Primary Count Site** is just below Enger Tower at the Rice's Point Overlook on West Skyline Parkway. This site is used on all days except those with east or northeast winds off Lake Superior. From 1st Street West, turn up the hill on 11th Avenue West, at 6th Street turn left to Skyline Parkway, and continue west a short distance on Skyline to the first pull-out just below Enger Tower.

(8) **The Secondary Count Site** is just below the Thompson Hill Rest Area on West Skyline Parkway and is used only on "cooler by the lake days," when winds are from the northeast off Lake Superior. To get there, exit I-35 at exit 249 (Proctor/Boundary Avenue). Proceed 0.4 miles past the south entrance to the Thompson Hill Rest Area to the highest point of the overlook/pull-off directly below the welcome building of the Thompson Hill Rest Stop.

(9) **Bardon's Peak Overlook** is another prime viewing area, located south of the Spirit Mountain Ski Area. Exit I-35 at exit 249 (Proctor/Boundary Avenue) and follow South Boundary Avenue to the intersection of S. Boundary Avenue, Mountain Drive (County Road 14) and West Skyline Drive. Turn left onto West Skyline Drive and proceed approximately 3.5 miles to Bardon's Peak, which affords an incredible, unobstructed view of the St. Louis estuary. Note that the parkway to Bardon's Peak is closed from mid-November until sometimes as late as mid-April.

PARK POINT/MINNESOTA POINT   SITES 10-13

DESCRIPTION   This area is one of the premier birding sites on the North Shore and should not be missed during either spring or fall migration. This six-mile long peninsula, referred to as "Minnesota Point," protects St. Louis Bay and the busy Superior Harbor from the forces of Lake Superior. Birding in this area during the months of May and September can be great, especially when foggy weather grounds spring migrants, particularly passerines. Fall probably outranks spring for both numbers of species and number of vagrants.

LOCATION   To explore this area, take the Lake Avenue exit from I-35 and follow Lake Avenue South, which turns into Minnesota Avenue farther down. There are several spots along the point, as well as before you reach the Park Point Recreation Area, where you may see a variety of shorebirds, gulls, loons, grebes, ducks and songbirds. You can park along Minnesota Avenue for most of its length. There are public access points at 8th Street, the beach access at 12th Street and 31st Street. If you pull in at 15th Street on the harbor side, birders have been permitted to bird from the Army Reserve Parking lot as well as behind the Bayside Market on 19th Street.

BIRDS   Numerous sites considered "birding highlights" in this area are detailed below with directions to each.

bird profile

Cape May Warbler

The Cape May Warbler is a passerine, part of the family of Wood Warblers that nests in open black spruce forests and fir/pine woodlands. In migration they can be found in pine forests, mixed forests as well as the shrubs of town parks. In spring, the male can be identified by a chestnut patch on the ear. Their diet consists mainly of insects, and feeds heavily on nectar in winter, often defending flowering plants. This bird winters south through the West Indies.

© MN DNR, Carrol Henderson

10 **Canal Park** Best for birding between October-December, this is a good spot to check for rare gulls on the breakwaters, to scan for jaegers, or to check for a Harlequin Duck in the shipping canal under the Aerial Lift Bridge. From downtown Duluth, follow the signs for Lake Avenue to Canal Park Drive, which in a few blocks leads to the park. From here you can hike back north towards downtown and then northeast along the shore on the Lakewalk.

11 **Hearding Island** in the bay along Park Point is an excellent resting spot for gulls and terns, ducks and shorebirds during spring and fall migration. The best place to observe Hearding Island is on the public land behind the Bayside Market. From Lake Avenue South/Minnesota Avenue, turn west at the stop sign at 19th Street, bear left and park alongside the apartment building parking lot. Use the path through the gate to the beach. You can also observe Hearding Island from the side of the road between the houses at 24th Street and from the Port Terminal.

12 **Park Point Recreation Area** is located 4 miles from the Aerial Lift Bridge on Lake Avenue South/Minnesota Avenue. The large parking area at the soccer area is a good place to park. The park begins at 43rd Street, and offers good views of the bay. On a good migration day, it is possible to see over 20 species of warblers on Park Point. Watch for shorebirds, jaegers, gulls, terns, Snowy Owls and occasional Gyrfalcons. You may see waterfowl rarities including scoters, Harlequin Ducks, Long-tailed Ducks, Red-throated or Pacific loons.

13 **Sky Harbor Airport** is a little airport for small planes and seaplanes, and also a great place for birding. There is a parking area just outside of the airport gate, and when visiting stay within the areas that are marked for hiking. Scan the runway for grassland species such as Horned Larks, pipits, longspurs and Snow Buntings. Watch among the dunes for just about any migrants, and search for owls in the pines. From the parking lot at the Sky Harbor Airport, you can hike the Park Point Nature Trail, a 2-mile one-way hike to the end of Minnesota Point, which overlooks the outlet of the St. Louis River. If you hike all the way to the breakwater at the end of this trail you may be rewarded with Whimbrels, a jaeger, or an unusual gull on the rocks.

14

HAWK RIDGE NATURE RESERVE   SITE 14

DESCRIPTION   As one of the premier migration sites in North America, Hawk Ridge was designated as Minnesota's first Audubon Important Bird Area (IBA) on September 17th, 2004. Unwilling to cross Lake Superior, fall migrating raptors use wind currents along the North Shore's ridges, which provide ideal flying conditions. Cold, clear high-pressure weather patterns with winds from the west/north-west bring the most migrants, but some birds can be seen on almost any day unless rainy or foggy conditions are present. The main overlook and the trails and other overlooks afford spectacular views of Lake Superior, the North Shore and South Shore of Wisconsin. Hawk Ridge provides excellent interpretive signs and a naturalist on-site during the fall migration peak periods.

© MN DNR, Carrol Henderson

LOCATION   From the east end of I-35, continue along London Road to 43rd Ave. East. Go north until it ends at Glenwood Street, turn left and at the top of the hill (0.5 miles), take a sharp right onto E. Skyline Parkway and drive east one mile to the Hawk Ridge main overlook. For a map and more information visit the Hawk Ridge website: www.hawkridge.org.

BIRDS   20 raptor species (15 of these regularly), have been identified migrating by the ridge during the fall migration season from mid-August to late November, as well as passerines such as warblers, thrushes, and waxwings. "Kettles" of Broad-winged Hawks are common in mid-September, with a record of over 100,000 counted on a single day.

Northern Goshawk

© michaelfurtman.com

Broad-winged Hawk

Other raptors appearing in notable numbers include: Bald Eagles, Sharp-shinned Hawks, Turkey Vultures, Northern Goshawks, Red-tailed Hawks, Rough-legged Hawks and American Kestrels. In addition, great numbers of Common Nighthawks are often seen in late August, and hundreds of migrating Northern Saw-whet Owls are banded each fall. Roosting Northern Saw-whet Owls, Long-eared Owls and Black-backed Woodpeckers can also be found in the woods along the road.

LESTER PARK AREA   SITE 15-17

DESCRIPTION   Lester Park offers an impressive network of scenic hiking trails and woodland birding along the Lester River as it tumbles its way down to Lake Superior. Just to the northeast of the Lester River is a roadway that goes through Kitchi Gammi Park (better known as Brighton Beach) along the lakeshore. This is a 150-acre park with roughly a mile of road right along the lakeshore, with pull-outs, picnic areas, and portable toilets in season. Farther east at the Lakewood Pumping Station, the lake and trees are worth a careful check and there are some small but interesting settling ponds to look over behind the building. This has been the site of some impressive counts of fall migrants moving down the North Shore between August and October in past years.

LOCATION   These sites are all located on the east side of Duluth. Directions for these birding opportunities in the Lester Park area are provided on page 23.

BIRDS   The forests of Lester Park are a good place to look for migrants in both spring and fall. Watch for conifer specialists such as Red-breasted Nuthatch, Golden-crowned Kinglet, Blackburnian and

Yellow-rumped Warblers. The mouth of the Lester River can be productive for loons, grebes and diving ducks during migration. Ring-billed Gulls congregate in Brighton Beach and sparrows and warblers can be grounded due to weather here and at Lakewood during migration.

15 **Lester Park/Lester River Mouth**   To reach Lester Park, turn off Hwy. 61 (London Road) at 60th Avenue East (3.5 miles from the end of I-35) and drive a short block to Superior Street, then turn right. After crossing the bridge over the Lester River, turn left onto Lester River Road. The parking lot is located roughly one block up on the left. There are two small parking lots just east of the mouth of the Lester River on Hwy. 61 that offer good scanning of Lake Superior.

16 **Brighton Beach**   To reach Brighton Beach, follow Hwy. 61 North and turn onto Brighton Beach Road just after the Lester River Visitor Information Booth.

17 **Lakewood Pumping Station**   This treatment plant is located about 2 miles east of Brighton Beach. To get there, continue on Hwy. 61 North. Follow the signs for the "North Shore Scenic Drive" instead of following the section of Hwy. 61 called the "Expressway to Two Harbors." Watch for the large brick buildings.

© michaelfurtman.com

Common Loon

STONEY POINT – FLOOD BAY   SITES 18-22

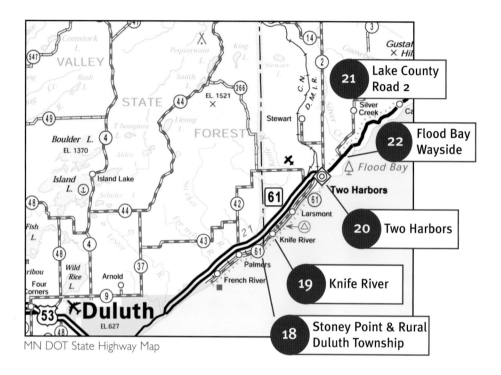

MN DOT State Highway Map

18 STONEY POINT & RURAL DULUTH TOWNSHIP

DESCRIPTION   Stoney Point is a broad point of land jutting into Lake Superior on the east side of a bay at the mouth of the Sucker River. It is noted as one of the best birding spots on the entire North Shore, offering good birding in the spring and fall for regular migrants and strays. During the breeding season the rural roads to the north of Stoney Point provide opportunities for grassland birds and wetland and shrubland species as well as all the common warbler species.

© MN DNR, Carrol Henderson

Northern Saw-whet Owl

LOCATION   Coming from Duluth, Hwy. 61 North splits into the "North Shore Scenic Drive" and the Expressway to Two Harbors. Follow the North Shore Scenic Drive for 10.7 miles north from the junction with State Hwy 61. Turn right on Stoney Point Drive, opposite Tom's Logging Camp. Stoney Point Drive circles the point and the Alseth Rd. bisects the loop; both return to North Shore Scenic Drive. The narrow strip of land lakeward of the gravel drive is public; the opposite side is private. To explore the rural roads inland from Stoney Point, go back one mile west (south) on Hwy. 61 and turn north on Co. Rd. 42 (Homestead Road).

In about six miles at the intersection with the West Knife River Rd., make a left turn and then a right turn at the next junction which is the App Rd. Proceed north for 1.5 miles until it becomes the Fox Farm Rd. and explore the habitats for a few miles farther north. Retrace this route south to one mile south of the West Knife River Rd. and turn west on Co. Rd. 40 (Hegberg Rd.). Follow it west for 3.5 miles and then south for four miles to Co. Rd. 43 (Lismore Rd.). Follow Co. Rd. 43 east as it zig-zags back to the Homestead Rd.

BIRDS   At Stoney Point many bird possibilities include: Horned and Red-necked grebes (spring/fall), Red-throated (spring) and Pacific loons, Long-tailed Duck, any three species of scoter, fall migrating hawks and a roosting northern owl. Fall also produces possible migrating Black-backed Woodpecker, Gray Jay, Boreal Chickadee plus regular flights of Rusty Blackbird, winter finches and sparrows. Many land bird strays have been seen here and past water bird records include: Yellow-billed Loon, Pomarine Jaeger, Laughing and Sabine's gulls and Black-legged Kittiwake. During the breeding season the best birding is inland along the rural roads in Duluth Township. At the open fields, stop and listen for sparrows. At the various wetland habitats, that include wet meadow, shrubby wetland, and some conifer bogs, stop and listen for Sedge Wren, Golden-winged Warbler and Le Conte's Sparrow. Some of these inland roads are dirt with little traffic so stopping and walking along the road at appropriate habitat can turn up twelve or more regular breeding warblers.

KNIFE RIVER

DESCRIPTION   Knife River occasionally hosts some interesting fall & winter species, especially gulls. In addition to the lakeshore, check the trees in town, particularly the mountain ash and conifers.

LOCATION   On Hwy. 61 North Shore Scenic Drive, 2 miles north of Stoney Point.

BIRDS   Check behind Kendall's store on west side of town where fish scraps sometimes attract gulls in winter (sightings have included Iceland and Great Black-backed). Visit the Knife River Marina (posted on Hwy. 61 in town), and scan the gravel beach and grassy peninsula for pipits, longspurs, and Snow Buntings in fall, and observe Knife Island where there has long been a Herring Gull colony, and a recent small colony of Double-crested Cormorants. Check the trees in town for Bohemian Waxwings and winter finches. Unusual sightings here include Boreal Owls, Townsend's Solitaire, Varied Thrush, Northern Mockingbird and a Scissor-tailed Flycatcher.

Two Harbors

DESCRIPTION   The "two harbors" of this town refer to Agate Bay and Burlington Bay.

LOCATION   The popular places to search for birds in Two Harbors can be reached from 1st Street, which is the last right turn off of Hwy. 61 along Burlington Bay, near the campground at the east edge of town. To get to Agate Bay, turn onto 1st Street, and then turn west onto South Avenue to 3rd Street, which leads to Agate Bay and the main harbor.

BIRDS On 1st Street, between 4th Avenue and South Avenue, search for Bohemian Waxwings among the mountain ash trees in late fall and winter. You may also find oddities here, such as Varied Thrush and Townsend's Solitaire. The cemetery along Hwy. 61 on the west side of town often attracts fall migrant geese, Black-bellied and golden-plovers, pipits, longspurs and Snow Buntings; also note the small settling pond near the southwest cor-

Bohemian Waxwing

ner. The ponds at the golf course in Two Harbors are just a short walk east and mostly north of the parking lot. There is the potential of shorebirds here, and later in the fall these ponds sometimes attract Snow Geese, with an occasional Ross's or Greater White-fronted among them. Birding the weedy fields between downtown and Agate Bay and north of the ore docks is also recommended. Search the harbors for loons, Red-necked Grebes, Harlequin Ducks, Long-tailed Ducks and all three species of scoter. It is also worth walking the trail along the shore to the east of the breakwater where there is a nice view of the lake from the flat rock ledges behind the old lighthouse, and a wide gravel hiking trail that goes around the woods of Lighthouse Point.

21 ## Lake County Road 2

DESCRIPTION Lake County Road 2 is a 46-mile tract of forested highway that penetrates the boreal forest. It is noted as one of the best roads to search for boreal species in Minnesota.

LOCATION (Mile 26.3) In Two Harbors, turn north off Highway 61 at the last stoplight on the east side of town. Three places that stand out for boreal habitat and birds on this road are 22-26 miles north of Two Harbors (the boreal forest around the Langley and Cloquet Rivers north to the junction with Forest Highway 11), another area 35 miles north of Two Harbors in the boreal forest both north and south of Greenwood Lake, and an excellent area north of the Sand River.

© MN DNR, Carrol Henderson

Black-throated Green Warbler

BIRDS Two miles north of Forest Road 11 is the White Pines Wayside, located within an island of virgin white pines. Listen for Blackburnian, Black-throated Green and Northern Parula warblers, Red Crossbills and other winter finches. Continue north, and listen for Northern Saw-whet Owls, which are

© MN DNR, Carrol Henderson

Evening Grosbeak

widespread and quite vocal on April nights. In spring also listen for Barred, Great Gray and Boreal owls. The real attraction of Lake County Road 2 are the Spruce Grouse, and this is one of the most consistent areas to find them, especially in winter. The best time to watch for them is in late December – early March, when they come to the road to pick at salt and grit. Most sightings are at dawn or soon after. The most consistent spot by far is just beyond the Sand River (some 41.5 miles north of Two Harbors). The grouse are most often seen within the first few hundred yards north of the river, or in the stretch 1.2 – 2.0 miles north of it.

22 **FLOOD BAY WAYSIDE**

DESCRIPTION This wayside rest is a good place for a view of Lake Superior, and there is an excellent beaver pond and cattail marsh between the beach dune and the Superior Shores Resort to the west of the parking lot.

LOCATION (Mile 27.6) Follow Hwy. 61 1.3 miles north of the County Road 2 stoplight in Two Harbors.

BIRDS During spring and fall, migrating shorebirds, sparrows and warblers are often found here. Vagrants seen here in the past include: Tricolored Heron, Great Egret, Western Kingbird and Grasshopper Sparrow.

GOOSEBERRY FALLS S.P. – WOLF RIDGE ELC
SITES 23-32

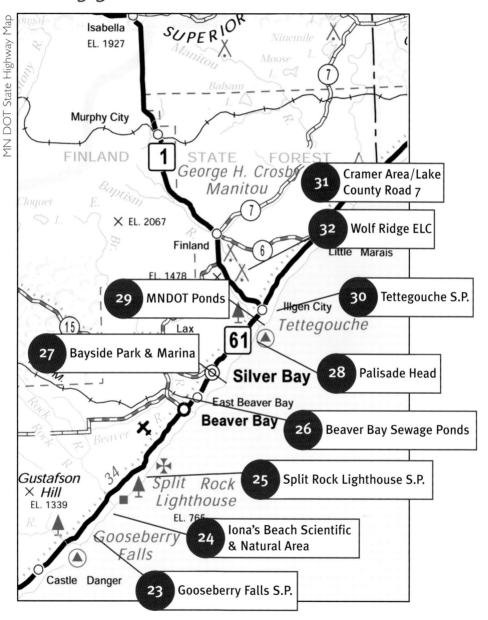

MN DOT State Highway Map

23 GOOSEBERRY FALLS STATE PARK

DESCRIPTION   The Gooseberry River drops through a series of spectacular falls and rapids to the rocky shore of Lake Superior. To get the most out of your visit, stop by the Joseph N. Alexander Visitor Center where you can find park information, interpretive displays, a park video, and the Nature Store, which has a bird checklist of the park. Or visit the Gateway Plaza for outdoor interpretive signs on area resources and history. The Superior Hiking Trail runs through a portion of the park.

LOCATION   (Mile 39) From the town of Two Harbors, follow Hwy. 61 north approximately 13 miles to the park. For more information call 218-834-3855.

BIRDS   225 species recorded, with 107 potential breeding. Similar to other parks of Lake Superior's North Shore, this park has its greatest potential for rarities in the late fall. Flycatchers, vireos, thrushes, warblers and sparrows migrate through the area in large numbers. On Lake Superior many types of waterfowl are present during various times of the year. Mergansers and many other species of diving ducks can be found on the lake. Gooseberry may provide the opportunity to observe winter birds such as Pine Grosbeaks, Common and Hoary redpolls, Red and White-winged crossbills, and the possibility of observing rare owls such as Boreal, Snowy and Great Gray sometimes exist in the winter.

© MN DNR, Carrol Henderson

Pine Grosbeak

24 IONA'S BEACH SNA

DESCRIPTION   Iona's Beach is a Minnesota Scientific and Natural Area. Geologically significant, the beach itself is made from a unique high berm rhyolite shingle. There is a parking lot, small boat ramp and loop trail. The east part of the trail goes through a stand of conifers and leads to a long gravel beach and one of the points. Another trail leads past the boat ramp to another point, and a smaller trail connects the beach to the boat ramp.

LOCATION   (Mile 42) Located off of Hwy. 61, between Gooseberry Falls State Park and Split Rock Lighthouse State Park. There is a sign on the highway that says "Public Water Access," which is the Twin Points Public Access.

BIRDS The woods and brush at Iona's Beach can be a good spot for migrating warblers, sparrows, and other songbirds during spring and fall. Brown Creepers and Golden-crowned Kinglets are often found in the red pine stand, and it is worth checking for roosting Northern Saw-whet or Long-eared Owls during fall migration. There are several mountain ash trees in the deciduous woods above the beach that are often used by flocks of American Robins, Cedar Waxwings, and Bohemian Waxwings during fall migration. The lake should be scanned for grebes and sea ducks during spring and fall migration.

© MN DNR, Carrol Henderson

SPLIT ROCK LIGHTHOUSE STATE PARK

25

DESCRIPTION Split Rock Lighthouse State Park is a famous tourist attraction along the rocky shores of Lake Superior; with excellent views of the lake and trails along the shoreline. This state park has been designated as an Audubon Important Bird Area due to the presence of Peregrine Falcon aeries. Birding on the grounds of the lighthouse itself can

Long-eared Owl

sometimes produce good results, especially in the fall, but birding within the greater state park area is much better.

LOCATION (Mile 45.9) On Hwy 61 about 20 miles north of Two Harbors. For more information call 218-226-6377.

1N DNR, Carrol Henderson

BIRDS 130 species recorded, with 77 potential breeding. Common Loons, Horned Grebes and Red-necked Grebes sometimes gather at the mouth of the Split Rock River in April to feed during migration. The woodlands are the summer home of more than 20 species of warblers plus Winter Wrens, Ruffed Grouse and Hermit Thrush.

Red-necked Grebe

26 **BEAVER BAY SEWAGE PONDS**

DESCRIPTION   Sewage ponds are a great place to search for migrating species.

LOCATION   (Mile 51.1) From Hwy. 61 in Beaver Bay, turn north up County Road 4. The ponds are 0.7 mile north of Highway 61.

BIRDS   Search the sewage ponds area for shorebirds and other water birds, and in the fall search the grassy surroundings for Horned Larks, American Pipits, Lapland Longspurs, Snow Buntings and Rusty Blackbirds. Open views here offer chances to spot migrating raptors in the fall.

27 **BAYSIDE PARK & MARINA**

DESCRIPTION   This park and marina offer good viewing of Lake Superior.

LOCATION   (Mile 52.4) Off of Hwy. 61, 0.9 miles north of Beaver Bay.

BIRDS   Scan the lake for migrating water birds and check the picnic areas for warblers, sparrows and other land birds. In the open parking lot area watch for larks, pipits, longspurs, and Snow Buntings.

Peregrine Falcon

© michaelfurtman.com

28 PALISADE HEAD

DESCRIPTION   This piece of land is a promontory that offers a beautiful view of Lake Superior. Palisade Head has been designated as an Audubon Important Bird Area due to the presence of Peregrine Falcon aeries. Use caution on the steep, narrow and winding road on your way up (closed in winter).

LOCATION   (Mile 57.1) On Hwy. 61, located 2.8 miles north of Silver Bay.

BIRDS   This is a site where Peregrine Falcons have successfully nested in past years on the cliffs below the parking lot. Some years the nest has been impossible to see, in other years it has been visible from the path that leads left from the parking lot. Care should be taken not to disturb the birds.

29 MINNESOTA DEPARTMENT OF TRANSPORTATION PONDS

DESCRIPTION   Marshy ponds are a type of habitat not commonly found along the North Shore. These small but interesting ponds have attracted several interesting migrants.

LOCATION   (Mile 57.6) On Hwy. 61, a half mile north beyond Palisade Head. Turn at the "Truck Station Illgen City" sign. The ponds are located behind the garage.

BIRDS   MN DOT ponds/open grassy areas are good for migrant Horned Larks, pipits, sparrows, longspurs, Snow Buntings, in fall; a few shorebirds and ducks sometimes stop here in migration; Marsh Wrens have been found during fall migration in the cattails, as well as Sora. Bald Eagles often roost and feed here in the winter, as the DOT often dumps road-killed deer here.

bird profile

Bald Eagle

The Bald Eagle, one of the largest raptors in North America, is listed as a threatened species in the United States. In the 1970s, populations suffered a severe decline due to habitat loss and reproductive impairment from the pesticide DDT, which resulted in thinning of eggshells and unproductive hatching. As a result of pollution-control efforts, breeding pairs of this species have increased tremendously. In Minnesota, the Bald Eagle has a had a strong recovery, with the population estimated at 1312 active nests in 2005. The adult can easily be identified by its large, dark body and white head and tail feathers. They nest in tall trees, usually near large lakes and rivers. Their diet consists mainly of fish, but also includes waterfowl, carrion, and small mammals. This bird is usually migratory in northern Minnesota but a few stay over in the winter.

© MN DNR, Carrol Henderson

TETTEGOUCHE STATE PARK

DESCRIPTION   Tettegouche State Park consists of over 8,000 acres with 23 miles of access trails. Rugged, semi-mountainous terrain surrounds four wilderness lakes on Lake Superior's North Shore. For spectacular views of the lake, be sure to hike the Shovel Point Trail.

LOCATION   (Mile 58.6) On Hwy. 61, the main entrance to the park is 4.5 miles north of Silver Bay. One good place to start is along the west side of the park. From Beaver Bay, follow County Road 4 beyond the sewage ponds and the County Road 3 junction, and in about 8 miles from Hwy. 61 watch for the public access sign at Lax Lake. In another 0.7 mile, park in the small parking lot on your right, the access point for the park. If you are coming from the north, this lot is 3 miles south of the County Road 4 – Highway 1 junction. For more information call 218-226-6365.

BIRDS   143 species recorded, with 85 potential breeding. Tettegouche State Park is probably best known to the birding community for its large population, possibly the highest in the state, of breeding Black-throated Blue Warblers. This species reaches its farthest northwest range in the United States in north-eastern Minnesota. These birds can be found most commonly along the trails leading to Mic Mac and Tettegouche Lakes. Twenty-three other species of warblers occur in the park, many of which breed each year.

CRAMER AREA/LAKE COUNTY RD. 7

DESCRIPTION   This side trip off of Hwy. 61 affords great warbler possibilities.

LOCATION   From Hwy. 61 at Schroeder, head north on Cook County Hwy. 1 (Cramer Road, across from the sign for Lamb's Resort). Follow to its intersection with Lake County Road 7. Park anywhere and walk along Cty. Rd. 7 in either direction. This road provides good birding all the way up past Nine-Mile Lake to Crooked Lake.

BIRDS   0.2 miles past Cramer on Cty. Rd. 7 has proven to be a reliable spot for Golden-winged Warblers in the open alder areas and Philadelphia Vireos in the taller aspens. Farther up Co. Rd. 7 near Goldeneye Lake, keep an ear out for Black-throated Blue Warblers, which have been located in the maple forests.

WOLF RIDGE ELC

32

DESCRIPTION   The Wolf Ridge Environmental Learning Center is a year round residential educational facility that is open to the public. Wolf Ridge occupies a diverse 1,800+ acres of the North Shore Highlands Ecological Subsection, including 100 acres of wetlands, two lakes, northern hardwood-pine forests, several areas of old growth yellow birch, white spruce and black ash, as well as some remnant white and red pines that still dot the ridgelines. Wolf Ridge has approximately 18 miles of well-groomed trails for hiking through varied habitat. Bird feeders near the buildings are maintained all year. Wolf Ridge has 2 decks overlooking the ridge and make a wonderful place to watch migrating raptors. A "MAPS" (Monitoring Avian Productivity and Survivorship) banding station is maintained from June through August. Call ahead for dates/times. Wolf Ridge is closed some weekends. For more information please call 218-353-7414. Visit www.wolf-ridge.org. Please check in at the main office on arrival.

LOCATION   (Mile 66) From Highway 61 in Little Marais turn onto County Road 6 for 4 miles. Take a left on Cranberry Road and follow the road to its end (this is the driveway). There are brown directional signs for Wolf Ridge on Highway 61 (both directions) and just before Cranberry road (both directions).

BIRDS   Through the MAPS banding station 96 different bird species have been identified. 32 of these are regular breeders on Wolf Ridge property. Highlights of birds seen at Wolf Ridge include: Yellow-bellied Flycatcher, Black-throated Blue Warbler, White-winged Crossbill, Northern Goshawk, Golden-winged Warbler (very northern part of range). Other birds include: Indigo Bunting, Red and White-breasted Nuthatch, Swainson's Thrush, Tennessee Warbler, Magnolia Warbler, Yellow-rumped Warbler, Blackburnian Warbler, Black-and-White Warbler, Canada Warbler, White-throated Sparrow, Dark-eyed Junco, Purple Finch, Pine Siskin, Evening Grosbeak, Yellow-bellied Sapsucker, Pileated Woodpecker, Least Flycatcher, Veery, American Redstart, Ruffed Grouse, Chestnut-sided Warbler, Ovenbird, and Mourning Warbler. During the fall migration it is easy to observe many hawks, vultures, eagles and falcons flying over the ridge.

bird profile

Northern Goshawk

The Northern Goshawk is the largest forest dwelling raptor in the Accipiter family of diurnal raptors. They nest in northern coniferous forests, and extensive conifer/mixed woodlands. Like the Bald Eagle, the population of the Northern Goshawk suffered a decline in the early 1970s due to the pesticide DDT. Their diet consists mainly of smaller ground dwelling birds and small mammals. This bird usually does not migrate, but has been recorded to winter as far south as northern Mexico when their normal supply of snowshoe hares, lemmings, and Ruffed Grouse are not plentiful.

© michaelfurtman.com

CROSBY-MANITOU S.P. – CROFTVILLE ROAD
SITES 33-46

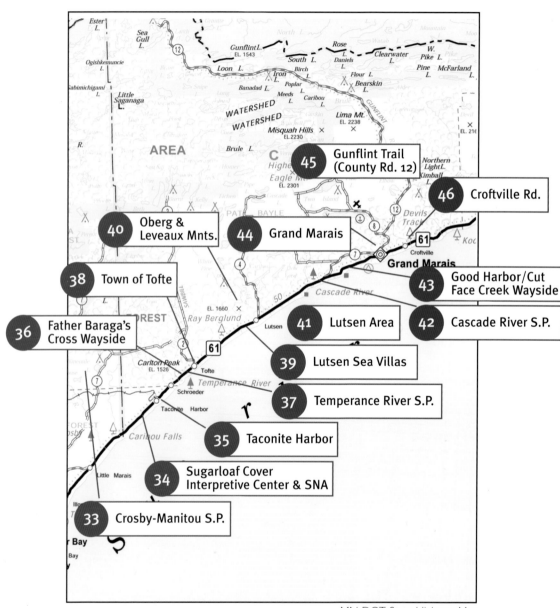

MN DOT State Highway Map

33 GEORGE H. CROSBY-MANITOU STATE PARK

DESCRIPTION George H. Crosby-Manitou State Park is a wilderness park of over 5,000 acres that stretch along the Manitou River. Backpacking and hiking trails cross rugged-rock and forest areas along the cascading Manitou River. The Middle Trail and the Manitou River Trail offer several scenic overlooks and plenty of good birding. For more information call 218-226-6365.

Common Redpoll

© michaelfurtman.com

LOCATION From the village of Finland on MN Hwy. 1, go 7 miles NE on County Road 7.

BIRDS 136 bird species recorded, with 84 potential breeding. A total of 23 species of warblers has been recorded in the park and this is an especially good place to find breeding Black-throated Blue Warblers. Philadelphia Vireos, Boreal Chickadees, and Yellow-bellied Flycatchers also occur in the park. Wood Thrushes, rare deciduous

Cramer Road and Baptism River

© Bonnie Hundrieser

woodland species in NE MN are often heard near the parking area. During the winter Pine Grosbeaks, Common Redpolls, an occasional Hoary Redpoll, Evening Grosbeaks and many Common Ravens are found in the park.

SUGARLOAF COVE INTERPRETIVE CENTER & SCIENTIFIC AND NATURAL AREA

DESCRIPTION For 30 years, Sugarloaf Cove was home to Consolidated Paper's log rafting operations. Now it is a place to learn about the natural and human history of the North Shore, with a State Scientific and Natural Area at its core. At Sugarloaf Cove, you'll find an easy one-mile interpretive hiking trail.

© MN DNR, Carrol Henderson

Wood Duck

LOCATION (Mile 73.3) On Hwy. 61, 70 miles north of Duluth between Little Marais and Schroeder. For more information call 218-740-2755.

BIRDS Check for migrating land birds along the trails and water birds in the cove.

TACONITE HARBOR

DESCRIPTION Follow the road down to the boat landing on Lake Superior for good views of the harbor and lake.

LOCATION (Mile 76.9) Located off Highway 61, south of the town of Schroeder. Heading towards Grand Marais, turn right just before the railroad viaduct at the sign for the Taconite Harbor Observation Area. Before going down to the boat landing, walk through the grassy and brushy areas to look for migrating land birds.

BIRDS Scan the harbor for water birds, and search the grassy clearings and parking lot area for sparrows, Horned Larks, Lapland Longspurs or American Pipits in October.

FATHER BARAGA'S CROSS WAYSIDE

36

DESCRIPTION   This wayside pullover is a good spot to view Lake Superior.

LOCATION   (Mile 79.2) On Hwy. 61, located 2 miles north of Schroeder.

BIRDS   There are mountain ash and crab apple trees in some of the yards leading to the wayside that are worth checking in fall and winter for migrant land birds such as Bohemian Waxwings, Townsend's Solitaire, warblers, sparrows, longspurs, and finches. Scan the lake for migrant loons, grebes, and ducks; Harlequin Ducks have been reported in the past at the mouth of the river during fall migration. It is worth scanning the lake here during fall and spring migration for scoters and Long-tailed Ducks.

TEMPERANCE RIVER STATE PARK

37

DESCRIPTION   The Temperance River is one of the most dramatic and beautiful streams along the North Shore of Lake Superior. There are 534 acres in this state park, composed of boreal woodlands and the rocky shores of Lake Superior. Unique falls, rapids, potholes and cauldrons are found along the Temperance River gorge as it cascades to Lake Superior.

LOCATION   (Mile 80.2) The entrance to the park is one mile north of the town of Schroeder on Hwy. 61 (about 77 miles from Duluth). For more information call 218-663-7476 or 218-226-6365.

BIRDS   105 bird species recorded, with 67 potential breeding. Over 20 species of warblers use the park for breeding. The Black-throated Blue Warbler can be found along the upper reaches of the Temperance River in the park. Great for late fall migrants and winter visitants, this is the spot of Minnesota's first (and only photographed) American Dipper record.

bird profile

Bay-breasted Warbler

The Bay-breasted Warbler is a passerine, part of the family of Wood Warblers that nests in northern spruce-fir forests and mixed conifer/deciduous woods. In spring, the male can be identified by a chestnut (bay) crown, throat, breast and sides. Their diet consists mainly of insects, with some berries. Large-scale clear cutting of Canadian boreal forest has caused a decrease in available habitat for this species, and pesticides to control spruce budworm infestations may have contributed to population declines. This bird winters to Central Panama and south to northern South America.

© MN DNR, Carrol Henderson

38   ## TOWN OF TOFTE

DESCRIPTION   Watch among the residential feeders, mountain ash trees and a small park where the lake can be scanned. From the town of Tofte, you can also follow the Sawbill Trail (County Rd. 2), which leads into the boreal forests.

LOCATION   (Mile 82.5) Heading north on Hwy. 61, turn right at the Godin's Sugar Beach Resort sign 1.7 miles northeast of the Temperance River, and this side road parallels Hwy. 61 in to town.

BIRDS   This is one of the best towns along the North Shore for Bohemian Waxwings, winter finches and rarities such as Mountain Bluebird, Townsend's Solitaire, Varied Thrush, Northern Mockingbird or Summer Tanager in fall or winter.

39   ## LUTSEN SEA VILLAS

DESCRIPTION   There are lots of mountain ash and spruce trees here worth scanning. It is okay to walk around the condos here, but be respectful of tenants / guests privacy.

LOCATION   (Mile 87) On Hwy. 61, 4.5 miles north of the town of Tofte (not to be confused with the town of Lutsen or the ski area). Note: These are private grounds. Birders should ask at the reception desk for permission to walk the grounds.

BIRDS   Watch for Bohemian Waxwings and winter finches. This is also a good place to look for rarities such as Townsend's Solitaire, Varied Thrush, and Summer Tanager.

40   ## OBERG MOUNTAIN & LEVEAUX MOUNTAIN

DESCRIPTION   You'll find great views, excellent birding, and good exercise here during the summer. Both trails are serviced by the same parking area. Oberg is the east trail, and Leveaux is the west trail. Bird species are very similar on both.

LOCATION   (Mile 87.3) Located off of Hwy. 61, along Forest Road 336 (also called Onion River Road) about 5 miles north of the town of Tofte. Watch for the brown Superior Hiking Trail sign and follow this short, 2-mile road to the parking area on the left. Walk back east across the main road where a hiking trail leads up the mountain.

BIRDS   Oberg Mountain is noted as being one of the best places in the state for nesting Black-throated Blue Warblers. It is also a dependable location for Scarlet Tanagers, Black-throated Green Warblers and Canada Warblers.

LUTSEN AREA

41

DESCRIPTION   Birding the Lutsen area will afford views of Lake Superior as well as birding in "pond" habitat, which is rare along the North Shore.

LOCATION   (Mile 90) After visiting Oberg Mountain, return to Hwy. 61 and continue 2.7 miles

© MN DNR, Carrol Henderson

Scarlet Tanager

north to the Poplar River. The Lutsen area has two spots recommended for birding; the Lutsen Resort and the Caribou Highlands sewage ponds. To get to the sewage ponds, return to Hwy. 61 and immediately after the river turn north on County Road 5 towards the ski area. Go 1.1 miles up 5, turn left at the wooden Homestead Stables gate, bear left around the stables, and park by the ski hill's equipment garage. From here, it's a short walk to the Lutsen sewage ponds. Note: The Caribou Highlands is private property. Birders should ask permission to walk the property at the main office.

BIRDS   Entering the town of Lutsen, turn right to the Lutsen Resort where there are feeders, a good view of the lake and the mouth of the river. At the sewage ponds, watch for rare shorebirds such Buff-breasted and White-rumped Sandpipers in the fall.

CASCADE RIVER STATE PARK

42

DESCRIPTION   This 5,050-acre park hosts spectacular falls along the Cascade River gorge as it drops to Lake Superior, as well as the Jonvik Deer Yard, the largest deer wintering yard in Minnesota. Cascade River State Park stretches for five miles along the North Shore.

LOCATION   (Mile 100.8) On Hwy 61, 8 miles north of Lutsen and 10 miles south of Grand Marais. For more information call 218-387-3053.

BIRDS   132 bird species recorded, with 66 potential breeding. Probably best in fall and early winter; anything is possible here. Watch for Bohemian Waxwings in the mountain ash trees during the fall and winter. The first record of a Harlequin Duck in Minnesota was recorded at the mouth of the Cascade River. The mouth of the river is also a gathering place for numerous water birds including Red-necked and Horned Grebes (mainly in spring), Common Loons and in the fall all three species of scoter can be found. Long-tailed Ducks are frequent winter visitors at the mouth of the river. Whip-poor-wills are summer residents and their calls can be heard frequently during June and July. In the fall, look for White-winged Crossbills in the white spruce trees.

43 GOOD HARBOR BAY & CUT FACE CREEK HISTORICAL WAYSIDE REST

DESCRIPTION   This wayside offers both great views and great birding possibilities. Cut Face Rest Stop is open only in warm-weather months. If gate is closed, one may park just outside of the gate.

LOCATION   (Mile 104.5) On Hwy. 61, located 4 miles northeast of Cascade State Park.

BIRDS   In late May, look for Whimbrels on the islands in Good Harbor Bay. In the fall, this is one of the most consistent places in Minnesota to find Long-tailed Ducks. Watch for large rafts of dark-and-light ducks, and for the spiky tails of the males. Be sure to also look for any of the scoters during migration, especially in October and November.

44 GRAND MARAIS AREA

DESCRIPTION   Grand Marais is one of the best birding spots on the North Shore of Lake Superior beyond Duluth. A small harbor, surrounded by varied habitat, is at the heart of downtown with residential neighborhoods immediately north on the hillside rising above Lake Superior. Public rock and gravel beaches, public park land, high-quality public forest land adjacent to the harbor and lake, a wooded point and a walkable concrete/rock breakwall provide excellent access to birding areas. This small community hosts two annual birding festivals. For more information contact the Grand Marais Area Tourism Association: 888-822-5000.

LOCATION   (Mile 108) On Hwy. 61, 4 miles north of Good Harbor Bay.

BIRDS   The Grand Marais Harbor and close-by shoreline has been host to more than fifty rare or unusual bird species. First state-record sightings for Rock Ptarmigan, Purple Sandpiper, Common Eider, and the first 20th century record for McCown's Longspur occurred here. Many species seen on Lake Superior also venture into the harbor, providing excellent opportunities for closer looks at Long-tailed Duck, Harlequin Duck, Surf, Black, and White-winged scoters, Pacific and Red-throated loons, and the more common migrating ducks, loons, grebes, and cormorants. In November and early December the harbor and its small marina have produced, along with thousands of Herring Gulls, sightings of Laughing, Thayer's, Iceland, Lesser Black-backed, Glaucous-winged, Glaucous, Great Black-backed, and Ivory gulls and Black-legged Kittiwake. Scan the sky for a possible Bald Eagle, or less commonly, a Gyrfalcon.

The west side of the harbor is public land, called the Grand Marais Recreation Park. At the very west end of the park is the Sweetheart's Bluff Trail. The park is excellent for spring or fall migration of both woodland and open ground species. Within the park (near the city water plant) there is a high rock beach, which provides an opportunity to view the lake and is accessed by a wooden stairway. Fall birding in the park offers the possibility of Townsend's Solitaire, Varied Thrush or Mountain Bluebird mixed in with more common migrating

© Elizabeth Wilkes

Grand Marais Harbor

thrush species. Fall brings flocks of ground feeders not only to the park, but also to all open sparsely vegetated areas around the harbor and include Lapland Longspur, American Pipit, Horned Lark, and Snow Bunting. Late migrants, especially warblers, sparrows, and flycatchers are often spotted in the park on grass or in the numerous mountain ash trees. Loggerhead Shrike sightings are rare and Northern Shrike sightings are expected, but there are records for both in the park. Records for Northern Mockingbird and Black-billed Magpie are primarily spring visits.

Summer birding in the Sweetheart's Bluff woodland offers nesting Merlin, numerous nesting warbler species, Ruby-crowned and Golden-crowned kinglets, nuthatch, flycatcher, and sparrow species on the high bluff portion of the woodland which is primarily boreal forest. Common Ravens nest below the bluff closer to Lake Superior.

The east harbor breakwall and wooded Artist's Point at the southeast corner of the harbor provide excellent opportunities to scan Lake Superior for loons, grebes, and other divers. The Artist's Point woods are unpredictable but can become a migrant trap during spring or fall. From Artist's Point the East Bay (Lake Superior) can be scanned as well as from the gravel beach of the East Bay.

© michaelfurtman.com

Merlin

The East Bay Beach is public land from Artist's Point to the first house and after that is privately owned. Birders should be sure to observe privacy requests. You can access the East Bay beach on a public street right-of-way at Wisconsin Street and First Street. There is a small catch basin pond near First Street that should be checked. This East Bay area has produced rarities including a spring Fork-tailed Flycatcher, a spring Lazuli Bunting and a spring Sage Thrasher (a fall Sage Thrasher was seen on the west beach). From late spring to early fall the rock beaches and associated puddles of the east breakwall are often places to spot shorebirds such as: Willet, Wilson's and Red-necked phalaropes and White-rumped Sandpipers being unusual; peeps, Greater and Lesser yellowlegs, Stilt, Baird's and other sandpipers being more expected. Watch for Whimbrel perched on wave-washed rocks. Similarly, the gravel beaches produce a variety of shorebirds from striding Sanderling to colorful Ruddy Turnstone. Both Marbled and Hudsonian godwits have been seen in the park west of the harbor's west beach. More common, however, are Black-bellied and American Golden-Plovers anywhere around the harbor on short grass or gravel beaches.

Check for all geese: A Brant is possible, Snow and Canada geese are common spring and fall, and look for the small Cackling Goose or an occasional Greater

Gray Catbird

© michaelfurtman.com

White-fronted Goose. Check for puddle duck species in the small marina. Keep your eyes open for big white birds, unpredictable but fairly reliable: in winter, watch for Snowy Owl anywhere around the harbor on rock or beach and, in other seasons, American White Pelican, Tundra Swan, an occasional banded Trumpeter Swan or visiting Mute Swan on the harbor, lake or East Bay.

Much of Grand Marais's small residential area is well-wooded and excellent habitat for a wide variety of birds. Walk north into the town neighborhoods and seek out the fall/winter flocks of Bohemian Waxwing in mountain ash and crab apple trees. Pine and Evening grosbeaks, Common Redpoll and the (less common) Hoary Redpoll, Pine Siskin, American Goldfinch, Purple and House finch are the winter feeder finches. At well-stocked winter feeders expect: Red-breasted and White-breasted nuthatches, Blue Jay, Black-capped Chickadee, Northern Cardinal, Hairy and Downy woodpeckers, Pileated Woodpecker at specially mounted suet and occasionally a surprise Red-bellied Woodpecker. Summer in town brings back several nesting birds not common in Cook County, such as Brown Thrasher, Gray Catbird, and House Wren.

GUNFLINT TRAIL (COUNTY ROAD 12)

45

DESCRIPTION   Along the Gunflint Trail and its connecting side roads, you'll pass through some of the best coniferous habitat for birding in the state.

LOCATION   The entrance to the Gunflint Trail begins on the east side of Grand Marais (Hwy. 61 North) as Cook County Road 12, and ends some 60 miles later at Gull Lake. The section of the Gunflint Trail, where birders spend most of the time, is between the South Brule River and Poplar Lake about 15-30 miles from Grand Marais. The last 8 miles or so

bird profile

Great Gray Owl

The Great Gray Owl dwells in the boreal forests, wooded bogs, and montane conifer forests across the northern U.S., Canada, and Alaska. Although rare in Minnesota, they can be common the northern woodlands every 3-5 years during "irruptions" when they have been forced south to find food. They nest sporadically in Minnesota and their nests are usually in abandoned hawk or eagle nests of sticks and moss, and occasionally on a stump-top. This bird winters in the northern U.S. and Canada.

© michaelfurtman.cor

of the Gunflint passes by some excellent spruce bogs. The recommended side roads for birding are Forest Roads 325, 152 and 315. The best of these is 152, or Lima Mountain Road. If you want to get out for a hike, a great place to explore is "The Fen," a floating bog and mixed forest located just north of Grand Marais on Cook County Road 64 ("The Old Ski Hill Road") as you head up the Gunflint Trail. Follow this road to the Superior Hiking Trail parking area, walk through the gate on the right (or north side) of the road.

BIRDS   As you stop to bird along this route, watch for Spruce Grouse, Black-backed and American Three-toed woodpeckers, Boreal Chickadees, Yellow-bellied and Olive-sided flycatchers and nesting warblers. Great Gray Owls are seen occasionally, and there are possible nesting Boreal Owls. "The Fen" has numerous nesting warbler species, Lincoln Sparrows, flycatchers and raptors.

CROFTVILLE ROAD

46

DESCRIPTION   This road parallels the lake side of Hwy. 61, and rejoins Hwy. 61 in 1.5 miles just before the Devil Track River.

LOCATION   (Mile 111.7) On Hwy. 61, look for the Croftville Road/County Road 87, about 2 miles north of Grand Marais.

BIRDS   Park at one end of this short loop and hike the road in spring or fall. Among the residential feeders and mountain ash trees you may find fall migrants or winter residents, such as Black-backed Woodpecker, Gray Jay, Boreal Chickadee, Bohemian Waxwing, sparrows, and winter finches. During late autumn, watch for Northern Mockingbirds and Townsend's Solitaires and other rarities.

© MN DNR, Carrol Henderson

Gray Jay

FIVE MILE ROCK – GRAND PORTAGE S.P.
SITES 47-52

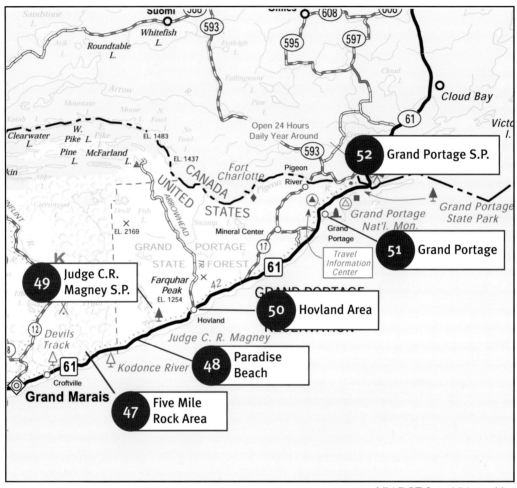

MN DOT State Highway Map

FIVE MILE ROCK AREA

(47)

DESCRIPTION   A good area to scan both the forests and Lake Superior.

LOCATION   (Mile 114.5) About five miles north of Grand Marais, this is a stretch of Hwy. 61 between County Roads 58 and 67. Make sure to park well off of the roadway here.

BIRDS   In the spring and fall, watch for loons, scoters, Whimbrel and Long-tailed Ducks In summer, listen for Whip-poor-wills at night and Philadelphia Vireos by day. This area also often hosts Bald Eagles, Double-crested Cormorants, and Herring Gulls. This is also a good spot to scan for waterfowl.

PARADISE BEACH

(48)

DESCRIPTION   A good place to view Lake Superior and small islands.

LOCATION   (Mile 123) Off of Hwy. 61, 14 miles north of Grand Marais. About 9.5 miles after the Devil Track River watch for Paradise Beach on the right (Note: no signs say "Paradise Beach").

BIRDS   From the gravel beach, Long-tailed Duck, all three scoters, Harlequin Duck, and occasional Whimbrels are often seen during migration. This is one of the most consistent spots in the state for scoters, and it is almost always worth the drive up here from Grand Marais in May, October, and November.

JUDGE C.R. MAGNEY STATE PARK

(49)

DESCRIPTION   Judge C. R. Magney State Park is a large wilderness park that stretches on the shores of Lake Superior and along the Brule River. The park consists of over 4,500 acres of mainly boreal habitat. Turbulent rapids and falls of the Brule River include the remarkable Devil's Kettle Waterfall. For more information call 218-387-3039.

© michaelfurtman.com

Greater Yellowlegs

LOCATION   (Mile 124) On Hwy. 61, 14 miles north of Grand Marais.

BIRDS   122 bird species recorded, with 70 potential breeding. At any time of year look for Black-backed and American Three-toed woodpeckers and Boreal Chickadees. Twenty-one species of warblers are present in the park, most of them breeding. Occasionally Black-throated Blue Warblers and Philadelphia Vireos are recorded in the park. Species present in the winter include Pine Grosbeak, Common Redpoll, Evening Grosbeak, and White-winged Crossbills.

50 HOVLAND AREA

DESCRIPTION   On the east side of Hovland (Hwy. 61 North), the Arrowhead Trail/County Road 16 heads north into Superior National Forest. Lake Superior is quite visible at Big Bay, five miles after Hovland. Please note that only the dock is public property, the rest is private land.

LOCATION   (Mile 128.3) On Hwy. 61, not far past Paradise Beach is Naniboujou Lodge on the Brule River (mile 124.2) which has a wide view of the lake, and in about another 4 miles is the town of Hovland and its Chicago Bay (follow Chicago Bay Road).

BIRDS   Scan the bay for loons, grebes, goldeneyes, scoters, Long-tailed Ducks and other waterfowl, and check along the road for migrants in May, September and October.

51 GRAND PORTAGE

DESCRIPTION   Located southwest of Thunder Bay, Ontario, Grand Portage marks the North Shore's terminus prior to the U.S./Canada border. Grand Portage is a small community on the Grand Portage Ojibwe Indian Reservation.

LOCATION   (Mile 144) On Hwy. 61 North, turn onto County Road 17 at the large gas station and casino entrance sign. Follow this to the left and continue on Cty. Rd. 17 to the fort. To scan the east side of Grand Portage Bay, continue past the fort ("Upper Road") and then turn towards the lake onto Bay Road, which will loop back to Upper Road. To get to the marina and the ferry that will take you to Isle Royal, turn right. Heading back on Upper Road watch for a trailhead to Mnt. Josephine (blue sign marker #183). The west side of Grand Portage Bay can be scanned from the Grand Portage Lodge and its marina.

BIRDS In May and again in September - November scan Grand Portage Bay for migrating waterfowl, loons and grebes. Bay Road is a good road for birding, and during migration land birds often stop along the shore here. In May and again in September - November, watch for migrating waterfowl, loons and grebes. The Voyager Dock area is another good spot to scan Grand Portage

© MN DNR, Carrol Henderson

Brown Thrasher

Bay from the East side. The overlook at Mount Josephine is a spectacular vantage point above Wauswagoning Bay. Sewage ponds are rare in Cook County, so don't miss the ponds that are located off Cty. Road 17. Watch for waterfowl, shorebirds and gulls. Please call the Grand Portage Lodge to ask if your group can be accommodated to bird on the grounds. Grand Portage National Monument is located in northeastern Minnesota's "Tip of the Arrowhead" within the Grand Portage Indian Reservation. The Grand Portage Trail is excellent for birding, with 192 documented species in the last five years. In spring and summer, watch the open field – unusual habitat in Cook County – for Brown Thrashers and other brush lovers such as the Gray Catbird and Clay-colored Sparrow. Birding checklists specific to the monument are available from the National Park Service. For more information contact the Headquarters: 218-387-2788.

bird profile

Boreal Owl

The Boreal Owl is a small, nocturnal predatory bird that nests in the mosaic of coniferous forests and muskeg in northern forests, including northern Minnesota. It is a tame bird, but very difficult to locate when roosting during the day. They nest in abandoned woodpecker holes or natural cavities with a well-matted bed of decayed chips and feathers. Their diet consists mainly of small rodents, but also birds. This bird winters in the northern U.S and Canada.

© MN DNR, Carrol Henderson

52 GRAND PORTAGE STATE PARK

DESCRIPTION   Grand Portage State Park consists of 300 acres of boreal forest along the Pigeon River on the Minnesota-Ontario border. The park hosts the largest waterfall in the state, High Falls, at a height of 120 feet. The park is designed for day use only.

LOCATION   (Mile 150.5) On Hwy. 61, about five miles north beyond Grand Portage you'll come to the border crossing. The park entrance is on the west side of the highway, just before the U.S. Customs Station. For more information call: 218-475-2360.

BIRDS   115 species recorded, with 76 potential breeding. There are only two trails in the park, but the one leading to the High Falls on the Pigeon River is a fantastic birding trail especially for warblers, with over 20 species having been recorded. White-winged Crossbills and Boreal Chickadees are often seen in the tall spruce tree near the contact station, and Merlins are regular nesters in the park. Below Pigeon Falls the river widens out into a number of rather quiet pools before flowing into Lake Superior. These pools are good areas for water birds such as ducks, mergansers, herons, gulls and kingfishers.

BIRD CHECKLIST FOR THE NORTH SHORE

This list includes species that are expected to occur someplace every year on the North Shore. See *Birds in Minnesota* (University of Minnesota Press) or *The Loon* (published by the Minnesota Ornithologists' Union) for appropriate seasonal occurrence.

This checklist was prepared by Janet Green and Jim Lind from published information, personal records and judgement. Birders are urged to submit significant observations to the Minnesota Ornithologists' Union at http://www.moumn.org.

Seasonal Status Key

P = Permanent Resident - present in the same area year round
S = Summer Resident - most species are presumed breeding
W = Winter Resident - present during winter months (Dec., Jan., Feb.)
M = Seasonal Migrant - season length variable by species

Abundance Codes (number seen at any one time)

C = Common – easy to find in appropriate habitat and season (>10 a day)
U = Uncommon – usually present in small numbers in appropriate habitat and season (1-10 a day)
R = Rare – difficult to find, present a few times in appropriate habitat and season (1-5 a season)
I = Irregular – not observed every year but expected to be seen again (once every 2-4 years)
a = accidental – has occurred but not expected again within the decade
nr = no records

	Season Status	Distributional Abundance (by County)		
		St. Louis	Lake	Cook
DUCKS, GEESE, SWANS				
Snow Goose	M	U	R	R
Ross's Goose	M	R	I	I
Cackling Goose	M	U	U	U
Canada Goose	S, M	C	C	C
Trumpeter Swan	M	R	a	nr
Tundra Swan	M	U	R	R
Wood Duck	S, M	U	U	U

	Season Status	Distributional Abundance (by County)		
		St. Louis	Lake	Cook
Gadwall	M	U	U	R
American Wigeon	M	U	U	U
American Black Duck	S, M	U	U	U
Mallard	S, M, W	C	C	C
Blue-winged Teal	S, M	C	C	U
Northern Shoveler	M	U	U	R
Northern Pintail	M	U	U	R
Green-winged Teal	M	U	U	U
Canvasback	M	U	R	R
Redhead	M	U	U	R
Ring-necked Duck	S, M	C	C	C
Greater Scaup	M	U	U	U
Lesser Scaup	M	C	C	C
Harlequin Duck	W	R	R	R
Surf Scoter	M	R	R	U
White-winged Scoter	M	R	R	U
Black Scoter	M	R	R	U
Long-tailed Duck	W	U	U	C
Bufflehead	M, W	C	C	C
Common Goldeneye	S, M, W	C	C	C
Hooded Merganser	S, M	C	C	C
Common Merganser	S, M, W	C	C	C
Red-breasted Merganser	S, M, W	C	C	C
Ruddy Duck	M	R	I	I
PARTRIDGE, GROUSE, TURKEY				
Ruffed Grouse	P	U	U	U
Spruce Grouse	P	R	R	R
LOONS				
Red-throated Loon	M	R	R	R
Pacific Loon	M	R	R	R
Common Loon	S, M	C	C	C

	Season Status	Distributional Abundance (by County)		
		St. Louis	Lake	Cook
GREBES				
Pied-billed Grebe	S, M	U	U	U
Horned Grebe	M, W	C	C	C
Red-necked Grebe	M	C	C	C
Western Grebe	M	R	I	a
PELICANS				
American White Pelican	M	U	U	R
CORMORANTS				
Double-crested Cormorant	S, M	C	C	C
HERONS & BITTERNS				
American Bittern	S, M	U	U	U
Great Blue Heron	S, M	C	C	C
Great Egret	M	R	R	R
Cattle Egret	M	R	R	R
Green Heron	S, M	U	U	R
Black-crowned Night-Heron	M	R	I	I
NEW WORLD VULTURES				
Turkey Vulture	S, M	C	C	C
HAWKS & EAGLES				
Osprey	S, M	U	U	U
Bald Eagle	S, M, W	C	C	C
Northern Harrier	S, M	C	C	C
Sharp-shinned Hawk	S, M	C	C	C
Cooper's Hawk	S, M	U	U	U
Northern Goshawk	S, M, W	U	U	U
Red-shouldered Hawk	M	R	I	I
Broad-winged Hawk	S, M	C	C	C
Swainson's Hawk	M	R	nr	nr
Red-tailed Hawk	S, M, W	C	C	C
Rough-legged Hawk	M, W	C	U	U
Golden Eagle	M	U	U	R

	Season Status	Distributional Abundance (by County)		
		St. Louis	Lake	Cook
FALCONS				
American Kestrel	S, M	C	C	C
Merlin	S, M	U	U	U
Gyrfalcon	W	R	I	I
Peregrine Falcon	S, M	U	U	R
RAILS, GALLINULES, COOTS				
Virginia Rail	S, M	R	I	I
Sora	S, M	U	U	R
American Coot	S, M	C	U	U
CRANES				
Sandhill Crane	M	U	U	R
PLOVERS				
Black-bellied Plover	M	C	U	U
American Golden-Plover	M	C	U	U
Semipalmated Plover	M	C	U	U
Killdeer	S, M	C	C	C
SANDPIPERS & PHALAROPES				
Spotted Sandpiper	S, M	C	C	C
Solitary Sandpiper	M	U	U	U
Greater Yellowlegs	M	U	U	U
Willet	M	R	R	R
Lesser Yellowlegs	M	C	C	C
Upland Sandpiper	M	R	R	R
Whimbrel	M	U	R	U
Hudsonian Godwit	M	R	R	R
Marbled Godwit	M	U	R	R
Ruddy Turnstone	M	U	U	U
Red Knot	M	R	a	a
Sanderling	M	C	U	U
Semipalmated Sandpiper	M	C	U	U
Least Sandpiper	M	C	C	C

	Season Status	Distributional Abundance (by County)		
		St. Louis	Lake	Cook
White-rumped Sandpiper	M	U	R	R
Baird's Sandpiper	M	C	U	U
Pectoral Sandpiper	M	U	U	U
Dunlin	M	C	U	U
Stilt Sandpiper	M	R	R	R
Buff-breasted Sandpiper	M	R	R	R
Short-billed Dowitcher	M	U	U	R
Long-billed Dowitcher	M	U	U	R
Wilson's Snipe	S, M	C	C	C
American Woodcock	S, M	C	C	C
Wilson's Phalarope	M	R	R	R
Red-necked Phalarope	M	R	I	a
GULLS, TERNS, JAEGERS				
Franklin's Gull	M	R	I	a
Little Gull	M	R	nr	nr
Bonaparte's Gull	M	C	U	R
Ring-billed Gull	S, M	C	C	C
Herring Gull	S, M, W	C	C	C
Thayer's Gull	M, W	U	U	U
Iceland Gull	M, W	R	R	R
Glaucous Gull	M, W	U	U	U
Great Black-backed Gull	M, W	R	I	a
Sabine's Gull	m	U	I	nr
Caspian Tern	M	U	R	R
Black Tern	M	U	I	nr
Common Tern	S, M	C	R	R
Forster's Tern	M	U	R	nr
Parasitic Jaeger	M	R	I	a
PIGEONS & DOVES				
Rock Pigeon	P	C	C	C
Mourning Dove	S, M	U	U	U

	Season Status	Distributional Abundance (by County)		
		St. Louis	Lake	Cook
CUCKOOS				
Yellow-billed Cuckoo	M	R	I	I
Black-billed Cuckoo	S, M	U	U	U
OWLS				
Great Horned Owl	P	U	U	U
Snowy Owl	W	U	U	U
Northern Hawk Owl	W	R	R	R
Barred Owl	P	U	U	U
Great Gray Owl	P	U	U	U
Long-eared Owl	S, M	R	R	R
Short-eared Owl	M	R	R	R
Boreal Owl	S, M, W	R	R	R
Northern Saw-whet Owl	S, M, W	U	U	U
NIGHTHAWKS & NIGHTJARS				
Common Nighthawk	S, M	C	C	C
Whip-poor-will	S	R	U	U
SWIFTS				
Chimney Swift	S	U	U	U
HUMMINGBIRDS				
Ruby-throated Hummingbird	S, M	C	C	C
KINGFISHERS				
Belted Kingfisher	S, M	C	C	C
WOODPECKERS				
Red-headed Woodpecker	M	R	R	R
Red-bellied Woodpecker	W	R	R	R
Yellow-bellied Sapsucker	S, M	C	C	C
Downy Woodpecker	P	C	C	C
Hairy Woodpecker	P	C	C	C
American Three-toed Woodpecker	M	R	R	R
Black-backed Woodpecker	M	R	U	U
Northern Flicker	S, M	C	C	C
Pileated Woodpecker	P	U	U	U

	Season Status	Distributional Abundance (by County)		
		St. Louis	Lake	Cook
TYRANT FLYCATCHERS				
Olive-sided Flycatcher	S, M	R	U	U
Eastern Wood-Pewee	S, M	U	U	U
Yellow-bellied Flycatcher	S, M	U	C	C
Alder Flycatcher	S, M	C	C	C
Least Flycatcher	S, M	C	C	C
Eastern Phoebe	S, M	U	U	U
Great Crested Flycatcher	S, M	U	U	U
Western Kingbird	M	R	R	R
Eastern Kingbird	S, M	U	U	U
Scissor-tailed Flycatcher	M	I	I	I
SHRIKES				
Loggerhead Shrike	M	I	I	I
Northern Shrike	W	U	U	U
VIREOS				
Yellow-throated Vireo	S, M	R	I	I
Blue-headed Vireo	S, M	U	U	U
Warbling Vireo	S, M	U	R	R
Philadelphia Vireo	S, M	U	U	U
Red-eyed Vireo	S, M	C	C	C
JAYS & CROWS				
Gray Jay	P, M	U	U	U
Blue Jay	P, M	C	C	C
Black-billed Magpie	P	R	I	I
American Crow	P, M	C	C	C
Common Raven	P, M	C	C	C
LARKS				
Horned Lark	M	C	C	C
SWALLOWS				
Purple Martin	S, M	R	R	R

	Season Status	Distributional Abundance (by County)		
		St. Louis	Lake	Cook
Tree Swallow	S, M	C	C	C
Northern Rough-winged Swallow	S, M	U	U	U
Bank Swallow	S, M	U	U	U
Cliff Swallow	S, M	C	C	U
Barn Swallow	S, M	C	C	U
CHICKADEES & TITMOUSE				
Black-capped Chickadee	P, M	C	C	C
Boreal Chickadee	P	R	U	U
NUTHATCHES				
Red-breasted Nuthatch	P	C	C	C
White-breasted Nuthatch	S, M, W	U	U	U
CREEPERS				
Brown Creeper	S, M	C	C	C
WRENS				
House Wren	S, M	U	U	U
Winter Wren	S, M	U	C	C
Sedge Wren	S, M	C	C	C
Marsh Wren	S, M	R	R	R
KINGLETS				
Golden-crowned Kinglet	S, M	C	C	C
Ruby-crowned Kinglet	S, M	C	C	C
THRUSHES				
Eastern Bluebird	S, M	C	U	U
Townsend's Solitaire	W	R	R	R
Veery	S, M	C	C	C
Gray-cheeked Thrush	M	U	U	U
Swainson's Thrush	S, M	C	C	C
Hermit Thrush	S, M	U	C	C
Wood Thrush	S, M	R	R	R
American Robin	S, M, W	C	C	C
Varied Thrush	W	R	R	R

	Season Status	Distributional Abundance (by County)		
		St. Louis	Lake	Cook
MOCKINGBIRDS & THRASHERS				
Gray Catbird	S, M	U	U	U
Northern Mockingbird	M	R	R	R
Brown Thrasher	S, M	U	U	U
STARLINGS				
European Starling	P	C	C	C
PIPITS				
American Pipit	M	C	C	C
WAXWINGS				
Bohemian Waxwing	W	C	C	C
Cedar Waxwing	S, M, W	C	C	C
WOOD-WARBLERS				
Golden-winged Warbler	S, M	U	U	R
Tennessee Warbler	S, M	C	C	C
Orange-crowned Warbler	M	U	U	U
Nashville Warbler	S, M	C	C	C
Northern Parula	S, M	U	U	C
Yellow Warbler	S, M	C	U	U
Chestnut-sided Warbler	S, M	C	C	C
Magnolia Warbler	S, M	C	C	C
Cape May Warbler	S, M	U	U	U
Black-throated Blue Warbler	S, M	R	U	U
Yellow-rumped Warbler	S, M	C	C	C
Black-throated Green Warbler	S, M	C	C	C
Blackburnian Warbler	S, M	C	C	C
Pine Warbler	S, M	U	R	R
Palm Warbler	S, M	C	C	C
Bay-breasted Warbler	S, M	U	U	U
Blackpoll Warbler	M	U	U	U
Black-and-white Warbler	S, M	C	C	C

	Season Status	Distributional Abundance (by County)		
		St. Louis	Lake	Cook
American Redstart	S, M	C	C	C
Ovenbird	S, M	C	C	C
Northern Waterthrush	S, M	U	U	U
Connecticut Warbler	S, M	R	R	R
Mourning Warbler	S, M	C	C	C
Common Yellowthroat	S, M	C	C	C
Wilson's Warbler	M	U	U	U
Canada Warbler	S, M	C	C	C
TANAGERS				
Summer Tanager	M	I	I	I
Scarlet Tanager	S, M	U	U	U
TOWHEES, SPARROWS, LONGSPURS				
Eastern Towhee	M	R	R	I
American Tree Sparrow	M, W	C	C	C
Chipping Sparrow	S, M	C	C	C
Clay-colored Sparrow	S, M	C	U	U
Field Sparrow	M	R	R	I
Vesper Sparrow	M	R	R	I
Savannah Sparrow	S, M	C	C	C
Le Conte's Sparrow	S, M	U	U	U
Nelson's Sharp-tailed Sparrow	M	R	R	I
Fox Sparrow	M	C	C	U
Song Sparrow	S, M	C	C	C
Lincoln's Sparrow	S, M	U	U	U
Swamp Sparrow	S, M	C	C	C
White-throated Sparrow	S, M	C	C	C
Harris's Sparrow	M	U	U	U
White-crowned Sparrow	M	C	C	C
Dark-eyed Junco	M, W	C	C	C
Lapland Longspur	M	C	C	C
Smith's Longspur	M	R	I	I

	Season Status	Distributional Abundance (by County)		
		St. Louis	Lake	Cook
Snow Bunting	M, W	C	C	C
CARDINALS & GROSBEAKS				
Northern Cardinal	P	U	R	R
Rose-breasted Grosbeak	S, M	C	C	C
Indigo Bunting	S, M	U	U	U
BLACKBIRDS & ORIOLES				
Bobolink	S, M	U	U	U
Red-winged Blackbird	S, M	C	C	C
Eastern Meadowlark	S, M	U	U	R
Western Meadowlark	M	R	R	R
Yellow-headed Blackbird	M	R	R	R
Rusty Blackbird	M	C	C	C
Brewer's Blackbird	S, M	U	U	R
Common Grackle	S, M	C	C	C
Brown-headed Cowbird	S, M	C	C	C
Baltimore Oriole	S, M	U	U	U
FINCHES				
Pine Grosbeak	W	C	C	C
Purple Finch	S, M, W	C	C	C
House Finch	P	U	U	U
Red Crossbill	S, M, W	U	U	U
White-winged Crossbill	S, M, W	U	U	U
Common Redpoll	W	C	C	C
Hoary Redpoll	W	R	R	R
Pine Siskin	S, M, W	C	C	C
American Goldfinch	S, M, W	C	C	C
Evening Grosbeak	S, M, W	U	U	U
OLD WORLD SPARROWS				
House Sparrow	P	C	U	U

RESOURCES FOR BIRDING & TRAVEL ALONG THE NORTH SHORE

PLEASE NOTE: The following resources are not provided as a comprehensive listing.

For more information on birding in Minnesota and along the North Shore

- *A Birder's Guide to Minnesota*, 4th Edition, © 2002 Kim Richard Eckert
- *Duluth Superior Birding Map*, © 2004 Duluth Audubon Society
- *Birds of the Superior National Forest: an Annotated Checklist*, Janet C. Green, © 2002 Boundary Waters Wilderness Foundation
- *A Birder's Guide: Cook County Northeastern MN*, Available from the Grand Marais Area Tourism Association: (888) 822-5000
- *Superior National Forest Birding Brochure (East Zone)*, For information contact: Superior National Forest Headquarters: (218) 626-4300 or www.fs.fed.us/r9/superior

For information on Minnesota State Parks

- Minnesota Department of Natural Resources: www.dnr.state.mn.us (Individual checklists available for each park)

For state records and recent bird sightings

- The Minnesota Ornithologists' Union: www.moumn.org (website includes updates to *A Birder's Guide to Minnesota*, as well as composite bird checklists for St. Louis, Lake and Cook counties, with maps on the distribution of each species in Spring, Summer, Fall, and Winter).

For information on travel, lodging & amenities along the North Shore

- America's Byways – North Shore Scenic Drive: www.byways.org
- North Shore Visitor – www.northshorevisitor.com
- Website for MN Traffic & Road conditions: www.511mn.org
- Explore Minnesota Tourism: 888-TOURISM (868-7476) or www.exploreminnesota.com
- Duluth Convention and Visitors Bureau: (800) 438-5884 or www.visitduluth.com
- Two Harbors Chamber of Commerce: (800) 777-7384 or www.twoharborschamber.com
- Grand Marais Chamber of Commerce: (888) 922-5000 or www.grandmaraismn.com
- Lake Superior North Shore Association: www.lakesuperiordrive.com
- Gunflint Trail Association: (800) 338-6932 or www.gunflint-trail.com